AF390528

TINY GIANT

A Collection

Jared Udsen

BookLeaf
Publishing
India | USA | UK

Tiny Giant © 2024 Jared Udsen

All rights reserved.

No part of this publication may be reproduced, stored in a retrieval system, or transmitted, in any form or by any means, electronic, mechanical, photocopying, recording or otherwise, without the prior written permission of the presenters.

Jared Udsen asserts the moral right to be identified as author of this work.

Presentation by *BookLeaf Publishing*

Web: www.bookleafpub.com

E-mail: info@bookleafpub.com

ISBN: 9789363311459

First edition 2024

To all healthy artists,
Everywhere

Come back

I used to walk with Death who now flies
And pecks all pink left in the sea
I watch from the bank,
Disappointment leashed beside Despair
I call to Death like I've lost a cat

 come back

It laughs in cold salt-air

I watch Death fly off with my family,
stubbornly
I know it will come back

FLY

Mr. Fly Died Inside
Where he missed his appointment
To be on the wall of
Occasional lovers

King Kong

I'll never be an ill-sick son of a
Who speaks softly around others,
but around those he loves
King Kong, crushing all
Your love looks like root beer
I watch you pour
As the man I want to be
Crossed the street

in looking for you,one

in looking for you,one Who (makes print
bigger on a diner Funny
you, yours and all of youse caught up in
some Christmastime shopping
for all your yous and yon'ts
i've found a me. I am not yet so
Wait

you in all (Ribs)

if you could see me just like i see you in all
i love you and love you more than i love you
i love you and you i love I know
you're more than all i love you more than
and all of you i love you now

carry me compared to the world

carry me compared to the world i am
nothing
love me compared to the world i am hope
i've had all of you and compared to the
world
you are fair
or should i say
id have all you again, without compare
e go
    no

No Rug All Rat

mouse how are
you   running in all the paint left
by the kids you

        must
        be a kid
, too

Perfect Peaches

Perfect Peaches
you will never be.
your label
 is different
from last
week.
those were
the
most
Perfect
Peaches.

sitting stupid
i could not spare the change
now i loathe yours

Mammoth Yale

mammoth went to Yale
i seen it with my own two eyes
pretty smart
career student been there millions years
like a few friends of mine
wonder what a mammoths grades are
strong in social weak math

Lizard Dream

Ask a lizard
Aren't you cold
Warm near the heart
The warmest part
Why do you choose
To paint
How fast you move
Cold-blood
Why paint me
In wicked blacks
Heart
You're no fan

tell me your name
if you speak
presumptuous - Me

CAVE 1

i know you crave
 a cave
where all the writing on the wall is yours
while what inspires you
is written miles away

who would win

i've never met a like you
promising veins beneath the streets
a real pulse
on whats really going on
when the lights turn on tomorrow,
i am power.
you say best friends
lets be honest
i carry you

Permanent Tomorrow

be warned:

there is a permanent tomorrow
some would call hope
it sits between the sky and sea
a great big house that homes all your dreams
                                    it is
bittersweet And
if you choose to live there

        a crow mid-flight can't look back on its
sorrows

Roads

There are things
Roads don't know and never ask
So before you go to
Your all-new life
Cleanse medicine on your mind
Consider
the price of gas

ducks.   in a row

all in all my ducks
are in a row except
for the ones that go
i pause
         the walk
to check the holes in the
 ground
with how it is
at least i care for ducks

A

Love ain't the type
to leave a voicemail
or ring bell-package at the door

B

I can't look
Height markers on the wall
All the years I didn't know

Horses First

Forgive me walking in
I know I'm late
but I'm here
I follow you now to Love, Anywhere
Horses First

time

he can't harness it
despitethe watch strapped firmly on his
wristhe's
aa plaything;
a kite in the windmouse in the mouth of
a catwho's learned sport

Oddbody

There's a mirror where he combs his hair
Before it's all on the tile
He brushes his teeth
Not all of them - only the ones in his mouth
Makes his coffee, and he, like his
Pours all around

It comes as no surprise to him
No, it has happened before
His body breaks out
All over the box he calls home
Looking for the nearest exit
His brain pleads to know
Where they wish to go

On the floors
There are fingers from his hands
Clawing at every door
As he moves back to slumber
Wishing his ghost would stop
Pulling him out of bed
As night dies, morning cries

He's back again

And Bravery

Out there is no where
I want to be
Need to and want
Never me
I get my boat
And bravery
I will catch
The biggest seen
But how does Man
Cast his great twine
When all good prairie
Surrounds
How they mountains
Dry his air

A Foot

i find myself
walking slowly
as not to disturb
the concrete

because
i'd like to believe
that the ground

remembersin sspite of us

i've never seen aprint without afoot

Unearth

Like bringing romantic
My heart jumps, ropes of arteries
double-skipped
I am an Earth, my chest and head two
continents
Separated by the ocean in my eyes
There is no peace, only war (only war
between them)
The river in my throat, a theatre of thunder
A battleground (between them only war)

Unbreak

When I found myself in cautioned trouble
Thought contorted, words a'blank
I knew what I was going to be
Saw my future in an instant
My tongue was with the cat
My mouth built a wall, bricks, unbreakable
Between my brain and house of teeth

slender

i slight a look down
cracked red, matched your lips
cracked - rust and kind
slender, how have you kept
your hands

a wonder to see,
to hold, just a moment
you pull me near, not close
what made those hands hold me now
"because"

i've seen those hands
push down the weak
and pull me up, like a test
you can hold me, i don't mind
slender
i don't mind a push

you brag and boast
yes slender, trample my plans
with your hands

Trees

those trees, my dad takes care of them
now he doesn't
that love i had, your paper heart in my back
stabbed
you've flown
to lands i can't
unless i taste
newspaper ink

"had"

inaccurate

www.ingramcontent.com/pod-product-compliance
Lightning Source LLC
LaVergne TN
LVHW010851200726
843508LV00012B/2853